The Dodo: The History and Legacy of the Extinct Fligh

By Charles River Editors

Frederick William Frohawk's illustration of a dodo bird in Walter Rothschild's *Extinct Animals* (1907)

About Charles River Editors

Charles River Editors is a boutique digital publishing company, specializing in bringing history back to life with educational and engaging books on a wide range of topics. Keep up to date with our new and free offerings with this 5 second sign up on our weekly mailing list, and visit Our Kindle Author Page to see other recently published Kindle titles.

We make these books for you and always want to know our readers' opinions, so we encourage you to leave reviews and look forward to publishing new and exciting titles each week.

Introduction

A picture of a dodo skeleton and model

"The Dodo never had a chance. He seems to have been invented for the sole purpose of becoming extinct and that was all he was good for." – Willy Cuppy, 19th century American humorist and literary critic

At one point or another, just about everyone has heard of the dodo bird, which is almost universally described as a cuddly, whimsical creature renowned for its alleged stupidity. This prehistoric avian had been known for hundreds of years before it was made popular around the world in Lewis Carroll's 1865 classic, *Alice's Adventures in Wonderland*. The character, the Dodo, satirized the author himself - according to pop culture lore, Carroll, whose real name was Charles Lutwidge Dodgson, regarded the dodo as his spirit animal due to his alleged stutter, which led to him often presenting himself as "Do-do-dodgson." Carroll was also a frequent patron of the Oxford Museum of Natural History, which served as a fount of inspiration for his memorable anthropomorphic characters.

The 1951 Disney animation, *Alice in Wonderland*, breathed new life into Carroll's Dodo, portrayed as a plump, peach-faced creature with a bulbous pink beak, clad in a purple waistcoat, a powdered wig, and a pipe dangling out of his beak. Like its real-life counterparts, the Dodo was depicted as a flightless bird who crossed paths with Alice, bobbing along inside of a bottle upon the open sea. Owing to its inability to fly, the Dodo uses an upside-down toucan as his boat, and the Dodo is being maneuvered by a green hawk furiously flapping its wings, serving as the boat's propeller.

The dimwitted, carefree dodo also made various appearances in film and TV shows over the years, such as Yoyo Dodo in the 1938 black-and-white animation *Porky in Wackyland*, the short-lived stop-motion animated series *Rocky and the Dodos*, and the 2002 animated film *Ice Age*, which depicts the dodos as a silly, clumsy troop of birds who fail to guard three small watermelons. Indeed, the dodo's presence in literature, picture books, music, video games, and general pop culture has been so prevalent that it has secured its own entry on *TV Tropes*, where it is infamously immortalized as the "Dumb Dodo."

This only scratches the surface of the string of misconceptions that has plagued the delightfully peculiar bird for centuries. Along with its stereotypical depictions in literature, film, and other mediums of pop culture, a number of idioms playing on the bird's alleged idiocy, as well as the supposed role it played in its own extinction, have become irreversibly cemented in the English lexicon. "Dodo" and the even less tactful "dumb dodo" are slang terms directed at dense individuals, an explicit reference to the bird's sluggish reflexes and supposedly pint-sized brain. One may have also come across a business venture or a fad that has "gone the way of the dodo" or is "as dead as a dodo," meaning that the venture has become defunct, obsolete, or a thing of the past, most likely due to reckless and half-baked business practices. The phrase "deaf to reality like a dodo" has also been thrown around quite frequently in recent years, used to describe individuals who are overly trusting and blissfully ignorant of unpalatable facts and ugly truths.

But were the dodo birds truly as simple-minded as they are often portrayed? And what were the actual factors behind the zany avian's extinction? *The Dodo: The History and Legacy of the Extinct Flightless Bird* looks at the origins of the bird, human contact with it, and how the species went extinct. Along with pictures depicting important people, places, and events, you will learn about the dodo like never before.

The Dodo: The History and Legacy of the Extinct Flightless Bird

About Charles River Editors

Introduction

   The Origins of the Dodo

   Endangered

   Too Little, Too Late

   Lessons Learned

   Online Resources

   Bibliography

Free Books by Charles River Editors

Discounted Books by Charles River Editors

The Origins of the Dodo

"On their left hand was a little island which they named Heemskirk Island, and the bay it selve they called Warwick Bay... Here they taried 12. daies to refresh themselues, finding in this place great quantity of foules twice as bigge as swans, which they call Walghstocks or Wallowbirdes being very good meat. But finding an abundance of pigeons & popinnayes [parrots], they disdained any more to eat those great foules calling them Wallowbirds, that is to say lothsome or fulsome birdes." – A Dutch report from 1598

The obscurity of Mauritius Island, located roughly 700 miles east of Madagascar, only heightens its mystique. Few are familiar this cragged, yet verdant island, a petite, pear-shaped islet floating upon the sparkling turquoise waters of the Indian Ocean, and even fewer can pinpoint its location when presented with a map. Those who have heard of this hidden gem, for the most part, know only of its luxurious beachfront resorts, hiking attractions, and botanical gardens.

While the island is indeed a perfect place for a romantic, yet action-packed getaway, it is the island's enthralling history, as well as its most famous resident, that makes it truly unique. And although it's not readily apparent, some say the island can be as fickle and unforgiving as it is breathtaking.

In the spring of 1610, Pieter Both, the first Governor-General of the Dutch East Indies and the namesake of the second highest mountain on the island, arrived at Mauritius, where he remained for close to five years. He hopped aboard the *Banda* and, accompanied by three other ships (the *Geunjeerde Provincien*, the *Gelderland*, and the *Delf*), departed from Mauritius on Christmas Day in 1614. On March 6, 1615, the four ships moored at Noordwester Haben (now Port-Louis, the capital of Mauritius) by Tamarin Bay. Superstitious characters later speculated that the voyagers had unwittingly brought aboard a hexed jewel or some other terrible artifact, buried within the heaps of gold bullions, gilded chains, diamonds, pearls, ivory, Ming Dynasty-era white and blue floral porcelain, pewter accessories, brass trinkets, and other artifacts spread across the ships. If not, they insisted, it was the island itself that must be jinxed.

Avinash Meetoo's picture of Pieter Both Mountain

Whatever the case, the treasure-laden fleet became ensnarled in a violent cyclone. The seafarers sprang into action at once and attempted to power through the blustering winds while setting their sights on the beach of Flic-en-Flac, but the *Banda*, along with the *Geunjeerde Provincien* and the *Gelderland,* were no match for the storm. As torrential rains and swirling tides sloshed aboard the three vessels, desperate men leapt into the churning waters in a bid to escape the swiftly sinking ships.

The *Delf* was the only one of the original four vessels to reach Amsterdam in one piece. In addition to the 45 lives lost, including Both, an estimated 223,262 guilders' (equivalent to 2,388.66 kilograms of silver) worth of cargo disappeared beneath the waves, most of which would never see the light of day again.

Dutch settlers and soldiers alike in Mauritius, as well as back in the mainland, were deeply rattled by the dreadful news, but Both's failed voyage was far from the first of its kind. The deceptively entrancing island had already brought about countless other shipwrecks and fatal misfortunes at sea, and at least 100 more in the future. Perhaps unsurprisingly, as was custom back in the day, Dutch sailors labeled Mauritius and its surrounding waters cursed, and they did everything they could to circumvent this route. It was only upon the discovery of the island's ample supply of ebony trees and its highly sought-after heartwood that the Dutch began to overlook this curse.

Some say it was this very curse that kept mankind at bay for so long, allowing the island's most celebrated inhabitants to remain undisturbed for hundreds of thousands, if not millions of years. To some, it was this supposed curse looming over the tantalizing island that protected them all those years, but it was also this same curse that gave rise to their sudden, meteoric demise.

These inhabitants in question were none other than the dodo birds, one of history's most controversial and intriguing avian species. Flocks of these beady-eyed, stubby-winged creatures, perched on clusters of beach boulders, watched, presumably with their heads tilted to one side, as ship after ship sank in the distance. This chilling visual itself seems to be a diametrical contradiction of the general public's view of the dodo birds, which are often regarded as hopelessly naive, endearingly dopey, huggable creatures. It is difficult to imagine that a bird as ostensibly harmless as the dodo would be associated with a place that attracted such danger and death, and yet, this was a place they called home.

A 1601 depiction of Dutch activity on the island and a dodo in the background

Somewhat ironically, before the early 19th century, the dodo was often brushed off by many as a folkloric, mythical creature akin to the unicorn or the Loch Ness Monster. This assumption stemmed from the lack of incontrovertible proof regarding their existence. Prior to the recovery and documentation of the bird's fossils and remnants, these surreal creatures were only seen in paintings and illustrations, not unlike Nessie, whose existence relies entirely on a blurry black-and-white photograph almost universally regarded as a fake.

On the opposite end of the spectrum were staunch believers in the existence of the dodo bird, and they were presumably pleased when they were eventually proven right. Before these flightless birds were officially recognized as real creatures who had been flushed out of existence, some of these believers pointed to conjectural evidence, such as their alleged appearances, mainly taking the form of flightless mythological avian humanoids in ancient folklore. Some forged a link between dodo birds and the Karura, a fabled creature from the Japanese Buddhist mythos depicted with the head of a bird and a human torso, said to be a fierce, fire-breathing god who feasted upon infidel serpents and dragons. Others proposed a connection between the dodo bird and the Egyptian deity Nekhbet, the bird-headed "Mother of Mothers" who watched over mothers, children, and the pharaohs, her bulbous, downward-curving beak somewhat reminiscent of a dodo bird's.

A statue depicting Karura

Could the dodo birds – or at the very least, their ancestors – have served as muses for these mythological creatures? And if so, does this imply that the dodo birds were not endemic to Mauritius, and that they were found in other corners of the world once upon a time? Today, those premises are now deemed to be quite a stretch, and historians believe other birds, such as the vulture in Nekhbet's case, were most likely the actual inspirations behind these mythological characters. That said, although the dodo birds probably played no role in the creation of these characters, the possibility that the species may have once existed in other remote, less-traveled islands and locales still stands. The dodo bird may be one of the most widely known prehistoric creatures today, but what scientists know about the flightless avian pales very much in comparison to the knowledge experts have gathered on mammoths, saber-toothed cats, and other ancient fauna, which accounts for much of the initial skepticism that surrounded the dodo bird's very existence.

An ancient Egyptian depiction of Nekhbet

To understand the origins of this paradoxically elusive bird, it's necessary to understand the origins of Mauritius Island itself. Interestingly enough, in recent years scientists discovered a "lost continent" buried underneath the volcanic island, which they believe was imperative in its formation. In 2013, a South African scientist by the name of Lewis Ashwal, along with his colleagues at the University of Witwatersrand, zeroed in on the disproportionately powerful gravitational pull exhibited by Mauritius Island, which was much stronger in comparison to neighboring islands in the Indian Ocean. From this, they concluded that Mauritius was seated atop chunks of a now submerged continent. Zircon crystals retrieved from the island's beaches have been dated anywhere between 600 million and 3 billion years in age, which astounded researchers since Mauritius is believed to be 8 million years old. Based on Ashwal's theory, the regular volcanic eruptions that shaped Mauritius over the years belched bricks of rock from the underlying continent, now known as "Mauritia."

Clement Larher's picture of part of Mauritius

Mauritia was originally attached to Gondwana, one of the supercontinents that formed following the fracturing of Pangea some 200-300 million years ago. In time, Gondwana suffered the same fate and split into Australia, South America, Africa, Antarctica, India, the Arabian Peninsula, and Madagascar. During this epic breakage, Mauritia, labeled a "microcontinent," no more than a fourth of Madagascar's land mass, found itself wedged between Madagascar and India. The microcontinent only began to expand when Madagascar and India began to drift apart, a transition spurred by volcanic eruptions and shifting tectonic plates, about 85 million years ago. The molten lava that spewed forth from these eruptions enveloped and buried the fragmented Mauritia, some of which were "recycled into the magma" that molded Mauritius Island.

The island itself, as previously noted, is a relatively young tract of land, birthed from cooled lava discharged by underwater volcanoes about 8-9 million years ago. The relatively freshly sculpted Mauritius, approximately 790 square miles in size, remained uninhabited by humans and therefore untouched for millions of years, allowing for the unhindered development of a variety of flora, aided by the fertility of rich volcanic deposits in the densely vegetated tropical island.

While these geological origins are understood, specifics pertaining to how the dodo bird came into existence remain a matter of dispute. Contrary to other famous extinct species like woolly mammoths, the unambiguous descendants of the Mammathus genus, scientists have been unable to comprehensively document the dodo bird's evolutionary process. As Leon Claessens, a professor at the College of the Holy Cross in Worcester, Massachusetts, explained, "The island has acidic soil, and is tropical and humid. It's a very unforgiving environment for [dodo bird] fossils."

Not long after the island popped up in the ocean, most likely during the Pleistocene Era, a flock of the dodo bird's ancestors, perhaps after losing their way, landed on Mauritius, where they gradually evolved in size and lost their capacity for flight. For centuries, scientists have been struggling to unscramble the identity of the dodo bird's ancestors. Early scientists speculated that the dodo birds may have descended from or were related to small ostriches, albatrosses, vultures, and rails, but the pool has since been narrowed down to the Raphinae bracket of the family of pigeons and doves. The connection was first made by Danish zoologist Johannes Theodor Reinhardt in 1842, who, upon examining the dodo skull in the Natural History Museum of Denmark, connected the dodo bird to common ground pigeons.

Reinhardt

Michael B.H.'s picture of the skull Reinhardt studied

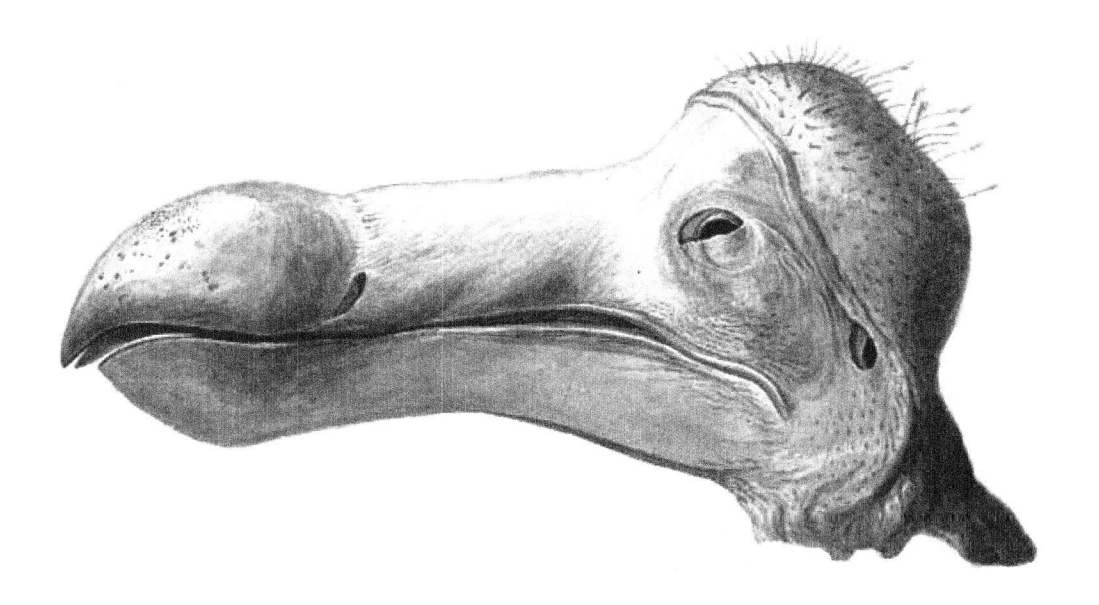

An 1848 depiction of a dodo skull

Reinhardt noted the anatomic similarities between dodo birds and pigeons. The skin surrounding the eyes of both birds, for one, appeared to be bare and hairless. Their foreheads, with respect to their beaks, were high, but with subtle curvatures. The placement of their low-lying, slit-like nostrils, found closer to the slope of their beaks, as well as the naked skin around the beaks in question, were features exclusive to dodo birds and pigeons. Both birds also had keratinous (a fibrous protein component in hair and feathers) tips on their beaks. If all that wasn't enough, both birds had comparable zygomatic bones, palates, halluxes, and mandibles, and their nostrils were bereft of septums (the partition that separates nasal cavities). In addition to the difference in size, the dodo bird diverged from the common pigeon in the short, seemingly stunted size of its wings, as well as its oversized beak.

In 2002, a team of scientists led by Oxford University's Beth Shapiro made a major breakthrough when they succeeded in identifying the dodo bird's closest relative, as well as its closest surviving relative: the Rodrigues solitaire and the Nicobar pigeon, respectively. This further validated their ties to the pigeon family. Like the dodo bird, the ancient solitaire, now extinct, once inhabited the neighboring island of Rodrigues (hence its name) and also laid one egg at a time. The Nicobar pigeon, a plump avian with a long ashy-black collar and distinctive iridescent feathers, is more of a very distant cousin, and researchers believe their evolutionary paths split over 40 million years ago. Scientists have since added crowned pigeons, native to New Guinea, as well as Samoan tooth-billed pigeons, to the dodo bird's mysterious family tree.

A 1708 drawing of a Rodrigues solitaire

Tom Frieder's picture of a Nicobar pigeon

Given the young age of the Mascarene Islands (Mauritius, Rodrigues, and Reunion Islands), all of which are less than 10 million years old, scientists have concluded that the ancestors of the dodo bird and Nicobar pigeon retained their ability to fly throughout the process of their gradual relocation. Their ancestors were native to other tropical islands and verdant territories, most likely in South Asia, and eventually wound up at this trinity of islands via a phenomenon known as "island hopping." The shortage of mammalian herbivores and immediate predators in these parts not only meant less competition for food, water, and resources, but also allowed for both bird breeds to swell in size. That reduced their wings to superficial accessories, as opposed to a useful mechanism for flight.

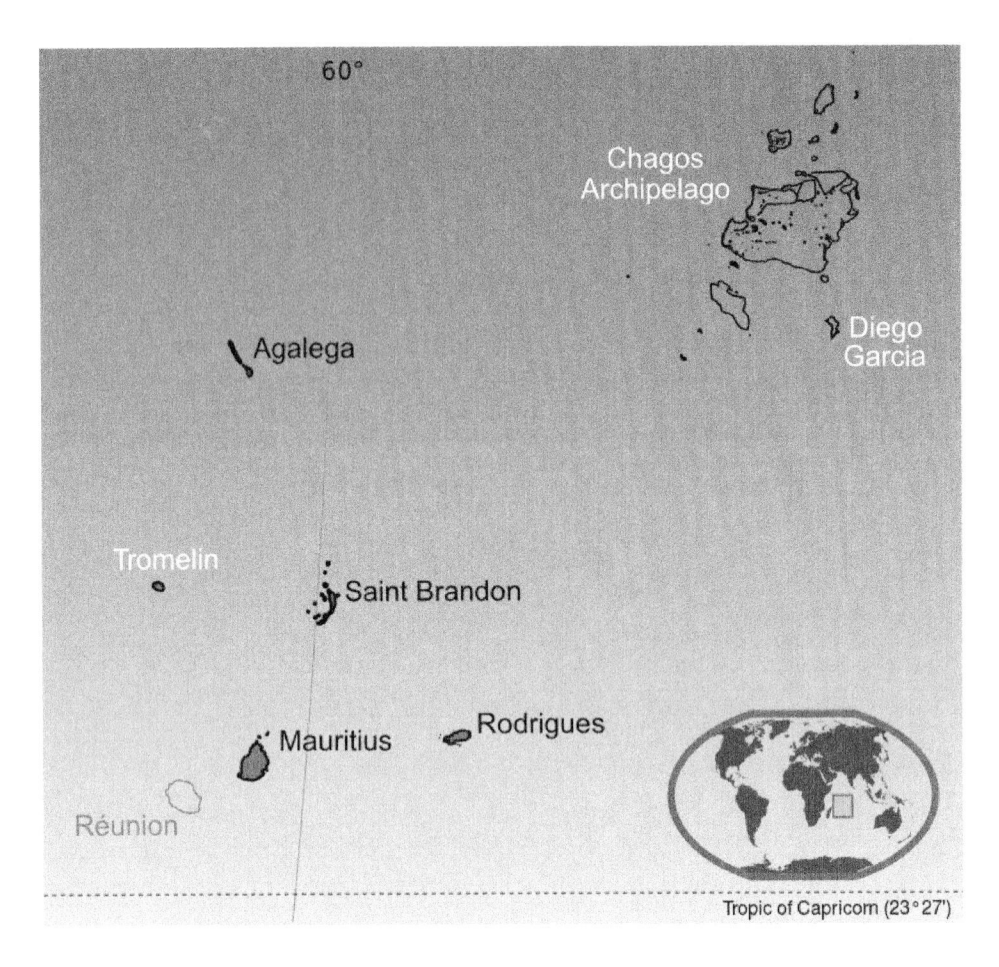

Yashveer Poonit's map of the islands' location

The curious lack of information on the dodo bird can also be ascribed to the fact that they managed to evade humanity's notice until the very end of the 16th century. To put this in better perspective, consider mammoths and other prehistoric creatures, whose existences were credibly documented in numerous cave paintings dating back tens of thousands of years, as well as the recovery of clothes, tools, weapons, and other ancient relics fashioned out of these beasts. Excluding their remains and the conflicting portrayals in paintings and illustrations, no cave paintings or similar relics of the dodo bird are known to exist, as Mauritius Island remained unoccupied until only recently.

Arab sailors were the first to document the existence of Mauritius Island, which they initially dubbed "Dinarobin" around the year 975. These Arab adventurers, like those who followed suit, chose not to settle and thus departed from Dinarobin shortly thereafter. These visitors to the island made no mention of the dodo bird or any similar creature in their chronicles, or at least none that may have mentioned them have survived.

Mauritius Island relapsed into virtual anonymity for the next 500 years, and it was only plucked out of obscurity once again in 1505 with the arrival of a Portuguese fleet under Captain Domingo Fernandez. Portuguese sailors returned to Mauritius in 1513, but again, failing to see any potential on the island, they also opted against settling. There were no overt references to the dodo bird found in the records authored by any of these Portuguese sailors, but some have suggested that the name they coined for the island, *Ilha do Cerne* ("Swan Island"), may have been a misguided reference to the flightless birds.

The absence of dodo bird references only makes this puzzling species all the more interesting. Considering that these birds most certainly did not appear overnight, one would think the sight of a sizable, comically homely bird confined to the ground would merit at least a fleeting mention in one of the journals. In addition to that, the dodo birds were supposedly tame and undaunted by humans, so there's no reason to think they somehow hid from the island's explorers.

Whatever the case, the dodo birds were finally documented by humans in 1598 when Dutch soldiers en route to Indonesia for the Second Dutch Expedition set foot on Mauritius' sandy shores. The expedition, jointly governed by Jacob van Neck and Dutch Vice Admiral Wybrand van Warwijck, was a smashing success, with the voyagers raking in approximately one million pounds of clove, nutmeg, cinnamon, mace, pepper, and other spices, netting their sponsors a 400% return on their investments. Their accidental brush with a never-before-seen creature rounded out their triumphant expedition nicely.

Van Neck

The vessel's detour to Mauritius was actually a spontaneous one. A contagious illness had broken out in the sailors' quarters and debilitated a number of the crew, so solid ground was needed, and fast. It was reportedly van Warwijck who spotted the island from a distance, and once the afflicted had been laid to rest on the beach, the vice admiral split the able-bodied crewmen into groups of three and ordered them to head inland and collect the necessary resources. The team headed by a Dutch sailor named Hendrick Dircksz Jolinck was the first to cross paths with the bizarre bird, and it was his description of the dodo that is now considered the first of its kind. They were also, it appears, the first to kill and roast the avian over an open fire. Jolinck wrote, "We also found large birds with wings as large as of a pigeon, so that they could not fly...These particular birds have a stomach so large that it could provide two men with a tasty meal and was actually the most delicious part of the bird."

Jolinck and his men, who were presumably full of glee and self-approbation after making this astonishing find, later presented Warwijck with the strange bird. He, too, made a clear-cut reference to these birds in his journal: "[The birds were] as large as our swans, with large heads, and a kind of hood thereon; no wings, but, in place of them, three or four black little pens (penekens), and their tails consisting of four or five curled plumelets (pluymkens) of a grayish color..."

It was then that the dodo bird was first formally christened, and fittingly, the origins of the mysterious avian's name remains a subject of debate. Although the Portuguese sailors made no explicit references to the dodo birds, excerpts from their records describe encounters with a kind of bird that may have been the dodo itself, which they may have mistaken for *pinion* (literally "small wing") or penguins. Moreover, some believe that the word "dodo" is a derivative of the Portuguese term *doido,* also spelled *doudou* and *dondo*, which translates into "fool," "crazy," or "simpleton." Vice Admiral van Warwijck called them *walgyogel*, also spelled *walghvogel*, meaning "wallow-bird."

Some etymologists have also attributed the word "dodo" to the Dutch term *dodaars* or *dodoor,* meaning "sluggard" or "knot-arse." The Dutch word is also the name of a diving bird known as the "Little Grebe," or the "Dabchick," most known for its clumsy gait. David Quammen, author of *The Song of the Dodo*, has also offered another possibility: the term "dodo" was simply an onomatopoeic translation of its two-note, pigeon-like call.

However the names came about, by the end of the 17th century, a dizzying 78 words and unofficial nicknames had been coined for the dodo. Perhaps not surprisingly, the bird also attracted its fair share of scientific monikers, such as the *Didus ineptus*, or "inept dodo," suggested by Carl Linneaus in 1766, as well as the *Gallinaceus Gallus peregrinus.* Fortunately for the dodo bird, the insulting name was eventually superseded by the more respectful *Ralphus cucullatus,* the Latin term for "bustard" or "hooded."

A 1638 painting of a dodo's head

That said, while humanity's first prolonged contact with the dodo birds can certainly be celebrated for the scientific knowledge that came with it, it was a blessing wrapped in a curse.

Endangered

"For food the seamen hunt the flesh of feathered fowl,

They tap the palms, and round-sterne dodos they destroy,

The parrot's life they spare that he may scream and howl,

And thus his fellows to imprisonment decoy." - English translation of a Jacob van Neck passage in *Voyage* (1598)

The varying descriptions and illustrations of dodo birds made over the years deepens the mystery of the dodo bird further, for its exact appearance is still somewhat open to interpretation. Only a handful of illustrations have been modeled after living dodo birds, with the rest often being warped imitations of original drawings. Generally speaking, the dodo bird was said to possess the following features: an ashy taupe plumage with a distinctive pattern resembling scales that extended to the upper edge of its forehead, topped off with a grayish, naked face; a smooth and broad downward sloping beak that bore either a pinkish, pale yellow, or light green hue; a fluffy tuft of dirty white tail feathers; short, orange-yellow legs and feet with four splayed claws (three in front and a thumb-like appendage in the rear) and sharp black nails; and yellow button-like eyes. On average, a dodo bird stood at a height of about one meter (roughly 3.3 feet), and their unique beaks measured about 9.1 inches in length. Some claimed certain larger male dodo birds were known to grow up to a staggering three meters (nearly 10 feet) in height, but these rumors are unsubstantiated. The average, turkey-sized dodo bird weighed anywhere between 22-40 pounds, but some of the plumper birds were over 50 pounds. Owing to the dodo's inability to fly, many early witnesses were hesitant to label their appendages as "wings," instead referring to them as "little winglets."

To say that a dodo bird was an unusual sight would be a drastic understatement. The Dutch sailors were understandably bewildered and even repulsed by these creatures, with many describing them as unattractive beasts. One unnamed sailor even went as far as to call the dodo "grotesque."

Despite the numerous depictions of these birds on the beaches of Mauritius, the dodo was primarily a resident of the forest. The island has various features, including rolling plains, mountains, and reefs, but the dodo birds primarily dwelt in the sweeping forests, replete with Pandanus and tambalacoque trees, located in the dryer coastal parts along the western and southern tips of the island. Remnants of dodo birds recently recovered from the highlands and nearby coastal caves also indicate that the birds were not averse to mountainous territories.

For a more poetic and vivid description of the dodo bird's natural habitat, one of the Dutch mariners wrote the following: "In the east, dense evergreen forests descended from the mountain tops to the sea, with massive ebony trees the home of gaudy colored pigeons and parakeets. Where the rainfall was not sufficient to maintain a closed canopy, the tropical forest gave way to a more open type of vegetation, a form of palm savannah, with glades studded with native palms through which lumbered hordes of giant tortoises..." Although they were not afraid of people, the dodo birds were never widely domesticated in any fashion.

A 1626 sketch of dodo birds

The harsh and often erratic weather in the region factored into the evolutionary development and behavior of these flightless birds. From November-March, the island is often battered by a spate of violent cyclones, relentless rainfall, and highly aggressive winds, which drowned and peeled off much of the island's flora, resulting in a scarcity of food. Due to the island's volatile weather patterns, dodo birds alternated between so-called "fat" and "thin" periods. The birds were at their chunkiest in the months leading up to August, which marked the start of breeding season, stuffing themselves with plenty of the kinds of greenery that thrived during these mild-weathered months.

During ovulation, female dodo birds developed a certain type of tissue inside of their bones that produced the calcium required for the production of eggs. Since the birds were flightless and had no need to defend themselves from predators, they didn't bother nesting in trees, or even in bushes. These birds produced and laid only one egg throughout their lifetimes, which made them exceptionally rare, and these eggs normally hatched after 46 days or so.

Frode Helland's picture of a model dodo egg

Unlike most other animals, both male and female dodo birds shared the responsibility of guarding the eggs, as well as rearing their offspring. The actual rearing of juvenile dodo birds, however, did not last long; the fast-growing dodo hatchlings attained their independence quite expeditiously, reaching sexual maturity anywhere around two to four months. If a dodo bird was born in September, for instance, it could grow to its full adult size as early as November, just before cyclone season. This rapid growth provided them with better chances of survival during the upcoming "thin" season.

The following extract, written by French explorer Francois Cauche in 1651, is the only surviving description of a dodo bird egg and the noise made by a dodo hatchling: "I have seen in Mauritius birds bigger than a swan...without feathers on the body, which is covered with black down; the hinder part is round, the rump adorned with curled feathers...In place of wings they have feathers like these last, black and curved, without webs. They have no tongues, the beak is large, curving a little downwards; their legs are long, scaly, with only three toes on each foot. It has a cry like a gosling...They only lay one egg which is white, the size of a halfpenny roll, by the side of which they place a white stone the size of a hen's egg...We call them *Oiseaux de Nazaret*. The fat is excellent to give ease to the muscles and nerves..."

Cauche's account may seem quite informative, but many of the details he included, such as the bird's lack of a tongue and its three-toed feet, have since been proven imprecise. For a time, experts wondered if Cauche had discovered a new species of the dodo bird, and some of them even provided a different designation for them (*Didus nazarenus*), but more likely than not, Cauche's confused description was a cross between a dodo bird and a cassowary. It was not unlike Cauche (or other early modern writers) to provide accounts with inaccuracies.

Recent examinations of dodo skeletons indicate that while their wings were not equipped for flight, the wings were not entirely useless. Dodo birds most likely relied on their stubby wings for balance, as well as mating displays, which included the "clapping of their hands." Even more surprisingly, subsequent studies of the skeletal structure of the width of their legs and their feet suggest that the birds were relatively fast runners.

Like any other bird, the dodo underwent cyclic molting periods. Whenever these avians began to shed their old feathers, calcium deposits embedded in their bones were activated so as to produce new, fresh feathers. This punctured their "internal bone walls" with indicative holes, a nifty trick found in numerous birds, in particular pigeons and penguins. The phenomenon probably explains the varying and occasionally contradicting descriptions produced by the island's human visitors over the years, as they would have encountered dodo birds at different stages of their molting cycles. There were some who claimed that the dodos had a smattering of dark quills rather than wings, paired with tails that had charcoal gray plumes. Others claimed that dodo birds had no feathers at all, and that they were simply coated in down, the layer of fine, wispy feathers usually found underneath the exterior layer of feathers. Molting phases usually commenced in March or early spring, beginning with the shedding of tail and wing feathers, but by the end of July, all its feathers would have regrown completely and as good as new, allowing for a fruitful breeding season.

An early 17th century painting of a dodo preening itself

A Dutch report originally written in 1631 but since lost remains the only account that details the dietary habits of the dodo bird, and it also hinted at the snappish and defensive tendencies of dodo birds: "These mayors (dodo birds) are superb and proud. They displayed themselves to us with stiff and stern faces, and wide-open mouths. Jaunty and audacious of gait, they would scarcely move a foot before us. Their war weapon was their mouth, with which they could bite fiercely; their food was fruit; they were not well-feathered but abundantly covered with fat. Many of them were brought onboard to the delight of us all..." Obviously, this directly contradicts the widespread belief that dodos were starry-eyed, awfully passive animals who did not shy away from humans.

In addition to ripe fruit that had fallen to the ground and was easily accessible, dodo birds were known to consume berries, seeds, roots, nuts, and bulbs. Although fundamentally, if not entirely vegetarian, like their relatives, dodo birds also possessed pescatarian tendencies, ingesting palm fruits, crabs, shellfish, and other aquatic invertebrates on occasion. When dodo birds fancied fish for a snack, they waded into shallow ponds and pecked at the water, described by some sailors as "strong and greedy hunters."

Sailors who were privileged enough to observe the dietary practices of live dodo birds up close were also flummoxed by their proclivity to knock back small pebbles and iron with ease. These pebbles served as gastroliths, commonly known as "stomach" or "gizzard stones," which rested in the gastrointestinal tract or muscular gizzard, allowing the toothless animal to break down their food and accelerate the digestion process.

There are virtually no coherent or conclusive reports on the dodo bird's behavior. Modern scientists today have yet to determine whether these avians were lone wolves or operated in social groups, but some witnesses characterized the dodo birds as monogamous beings who were supposedly "loyal to [their] mates and dedicated to [their] hatchlings."

As previously mentioned, the manner in which the dodo birds confronted humans and other potential predators remains a matter of contention. To some, they were gullible creatures whose lack of fear of human hunters and the concept of danger in general, as well as their lazy dispositions, made them easy targets. In the same breath, these people described dodo birds as amusingly uncoordinated and graceless animals. According to one account, a group of mariners watched as one dodo bird in particular made an attempt to scramble to safety, only to have its speed hampered by the friction of its fleshy stomach dragging across the ground.

Contradictory accounts, on the other hand, such as the 1631 account above, described the dodo bird as a relatively arrogant, somewhat brutish, and periodically vindictive creature that was not opposed to putting its sharp beak and talons to use should the situation call for it. Some dodo birds, when confronted hunters, delivered "fearsome bites" with their "powerful beaks" that left raw, bloody gashes and severe, pulsing wounds. Dodo birds, like most other animals, were intensely protective of their young and became hostile whenever they deemed their hatchlings to be at risk. Admiral Pieter Willem Verhoeven learned this lesson the hard way when he got much too close to a nest for a mother dodo bird's liking. He was "pecked mighty hard" and chased off by the wrathful creature.

Still, dodo birds were generally less aggressive than the solitaires in Rodrigues, and for the most part, they maintained harmonious relationships with their counterparts. Territorial battles, mating standoffs, and other disputes were considered a rarity.

While precious little is known about certain details regarding the dodo bird's lifestyle and behavioral tendencies – researchers don't have the slightest clue what their life expectancy was - scientists have recently succeeded in figuring out their relationship with the tambalacoque tree, or *Sideroxylon grandiflorum,* also known as the "dodo tree." These one-of-a-kind trees, also endemic to the island, were the sources of the dodo bird's favorite food: a type of fruit that resembled a juicy peach in both taste and appearance.

A young dodo tree

Towards the end of the 1970s, a young American botanist and avian ecologist named Stanley Temple sounded the alarm upon discovering the lack of tambalacoque trees in Mauritius at the time. Only 13 tree specimens, estimated to be 300 years old, remained, which he attributed to the disappearance of dodo birds. According to Temple's theory, the dodo bird and the tambalacoque tree had a strict symbiosis, mutually reaping benefits from one another. When dodo birds devoured the fruits of tambalacoque trees, they ingested, along with the flesh, its seeds, similar to peach pits, which were coated in a hard and fibrous coating known as "endocarp." The endocarp, or shell of the seed, Temple speculated, was specifically designed by evolution with the dodo bird in mind to protect the seed as it traveled through the gizzard of the avian. The germination was entirely reliant on the endocarp-laminated seeds successfully breaking down in the gizzard and stomach acids of a dodo bird, which allowed for water to pierce through the seed, making it ready for the germination process following its release. Plainly put, without the dodo bird, there would be no tambalacoque trees.

Fortunately for the tambalacoque tree, Temple's theory has been debunked by scientists who found a correlation, but not causation in the relationship between the flightless avian and the tree. Mauritius tortoises are also equipped with the ability to disperse germination-ready tambalacoque seeds. Additionally, more tambalacoque trees, including juveniles, have since been located, which indicates that these trees were not solely dependent on dodo birds.

All things considered, dodo birds led relaxed lives, mostly thanks to the lack of wild predators on the island. They peacefully coexisted with other easygoing, non-confrontational animals found in Mauritius, such as but not limited to turtles, fish, and doves. The absence of predators completely eliminated their natural guard, which explains the fearlessness (often mistaken for foolhardiness) that the dodo birds exhibited towards the humans.

The dodo bird descriptions compiled by Vice Admiral Wybrand van Warwijck and his crew were first published in a brief treatise entitled "A True Report" in 1599. Inserted into this treatise was an intricate copper engraving that captured the first-ever likeness of the dodo bird, as well as a glimpse into the activities of the Dutch sailors. The bulk of the existing knowledge on dodo birds today continues to be based off the reports drafted by Warwijck and his men.

The dodo bird made another appearance in a series of documents released in 1602, which also included the first rough sketches of the fascinating flightless bird. The historic rendering was the work of a veteran artist named Joris Joostensz Laerle, who had been invited aboard the Mauritius-bound voyage of the Dutch East India Company ship *Gelderland*, spearheaded by an Admiral Wolphert Harmenszoon that year. The caption underneath Laerle's sketches provided additional details: "These birds are caught on the island of Mauritius in large quantities because they are unable to fly. They are good food and often have stones in their stomachs, as big as eggs, sometimes bigger or smaller, and are called '*griffeendt*,' or '*Kermis [*geese*]*'." Laerle's illustrations are now considered to be the only indisputable renderings of live dodo birds in existence.

The 1601 sketches of living and dead dodo birds

That same year, the dodo bird was referenced again in the journal kept by Captain Willem Van West-Zanen aboard the *Bruin-Vis*. The account reported that around 25 dodo birds had been slaughtered to feed the sailors, and they were supposedly so rotund and meaty that the men could barely finish two birds in one sitting, so the leftover birds were thoroughly salted and preserved for later dates. The entry was accompanied by an exquisite engraving, aptly entitled "A Hunt on Dodos for Food," which was carved by an H. Soete Boom. The metrical inscription underneath the engraving read:

"Nourishment men seek here and flesh of't plumed creatures

Of the palm trees' sap, the dodos round of hinds

All while men the parrot hold that he pipes and shrieks

And cause that others besides also befall the coops..."

In 1619, the scientific and seafaring community became abuzz with excitement when rumors of white dodo birds on Reunion Island began to circulate. These rumors came on the heels of Willem Ysbrandtszoon Bontekoe's (a skipper in the Dutch East India Company) stop at Reunion, a fortuitous event prompted by strong winds and bad weather. Like Vice Admiral van Warwijck, Bontekoe chose to alight at Reunion Island to allow his sailors, struck with motion sickness and other ailments, to recuperate on solid ground. Much to Bontekoe's amazement, he came across a number of enchanting tropical birds, among which were "[white] dodos that had small wings yet could not fly...[and] were so fat they could [scarcely] move...[resorting to dragging] their back-ends on the ground." Six years later, Dutch Chief Officer J. Tatton also reported sightings of a white, thickset bird with non-functioning wings, or as he put it, "a great fowl the bigness of a turkey, very fat, and so short-winged that they cannot fly, being white."

Although the sightings of these mystifying all-white dodos, reported by highly-esteemed officers well-respected in their circles, were taken seriously for some time, the lack of subsequent reports or similar sightings in the decades that followed eventually led experts to discredit the existence of the white dodos. The albino dodo birds of Reunion Island are now regarded as either pure myth or a misinterpretation of other white, flightless birds such as the Reunion solitaire or the Reunion ibis. Paintings of these white dodos, produced by Dutch artists Pieter Holsteyn II and Pieter Withoos, have been similarly cast aside.

In no uncertain terms, the colonization of Mauritius Island, which unequivocally affected the dodo's natural habitat and robbed them of essential resources, spelled the beginning of the flightless avian's undoing. Almost immediately after the accidental discovery of the dodo bird in 1598, the Dutch mariners unofficially planted their flag on the island, which they named after Prince Maurits of Nassau. The enterprising Dutch East India Company dispatched Simons Gooyer to Mauritius later that year, and he was then crowned the first governor, or *Opperhoofd*, of Dutch Mauritius, along with a modest band of 25 settlers. Following the establishment of the Dutch camp, settlers began to receive cargo ships hailing from the motherland that consistently cast their anchor along the island shore to load up on and replenish the provisions of those stationed at Mauritius.

Prince Maurits of Nassau

Be that as it may, the Dutch only officially acquired the island in 1638, which was formally established as a penal colony financed by the Dutch East India Company. The prosperous corporation took note of the island's business potential, particularly the abundant resources on the island that past visitors failed to recognize, and its location allowed them to bolster and better safeguard their trade routes. Adriaan van der Stel arrived at Mauritius two years later, accompanied by 70 other settlers, and was crowned *Opperhoofd* of the island colony. 40 of the 70 settlers who joined van der Stel at Mauritius were sickly, feeble individuals who hoped to restore their health on the island. During this time, Dutch settlers also imported throngs of Madagascan, Indian, and Chinese slaves and manual laborers.

The colonizers' hunting of the dodo birds in Mauritius was the most salient of all the major changes the birds confronted. A woodcutting dating back to 1604 illustrated the dodo's new plight. Some sailors are seen luring gray parrots and dodo birds onto the shore, seizing the birds by the wings to prevent their escape. Others wielded sticks and clubs over their heads, striking a troupe of the startled avians. Two heaps of dead dodo birds and parrots, stiff as a board, were strewn across the sand. On the right-hand side of the colorized woodcutting are Dutch ships by the shore, which symbolized the coming of even more death and despair.

The settlers were irresponsibly impulsive and imprudent in their slaughter of the island's dodo birds. According to the one account mentioned above, as many as 25 of these poor creatures were butchered in a single stroke, and reports gathered in the ensuing decades implied that the dodos were regularly slaughtered and consumed by the Dutch settlers. A passage from a report published in mid-August 1673, for instance, revealed that at least half a dozen dodos were killed and made into meals for *Opperhoofd* Hubert Hugo.

Today, some historians believe that the accounts regarding the merciless slaughter of Mauritius' dodo birds were overexaggerated, and that the dodo birds may not have been as widely and vigorously hunted and eaten as previously thought. For one thing, most dodo birds were far leaner than artistic depictions and were thus sinewy and less appetizing than they are typically depicted. As previously mentioned, the nickname *walghvoghel,* conceived by Vice Admiral van Warwijck, also translated to "tasteless" or "sickly bird," with flesh supposedly so greasy and cloying that many of the sailors who sunk their teeth into it broke out in sweats and began to retch and heave.

On that note, although it was Warwijck who came up with the unflattering name, he appeared to be fairly partial to the taste of dodo bird meat. Indeed, he mentioned his preference for blue and gray parrots, as well as other poultry on the island, and he complained about the difficulty of cooking the dodo bird thoroughly: "These [dodo] birds we took [sic] a certain amount, together with some turtles and other birds. We boiled this bird but he was so tough that we could not boil it enough, and we ate it only half-baked." That said, he added, "Nevertheless, their belly and breast were of a pleasant flavor and were easily masticated." To sum it up, while dodo birds made for mediocre-tasting suppers at best and were possibly only hunted to a moderate extent, they were nonetheless targeted by hunters, which most definitely played a hand in the decline of the island's dodo population.

As it turns out, the foreign plants and animals that the settlers brought to the island in droves posed a far more immediate threat. Along with the settlers, slaves, and laborers that poured into Mauritius, mariners stocked their ships with scores of domesticated animals from home, including felines, monkeys, pigs, goats, sheep, rabbits, stags, ducks, geese, and lava deer. These invasive species, intended as additional food supplies for the settlers and passing ships, essentially ran amok on Mauritius.

To be fair, the Dutch colonizers were not the only ones to blame for the abrupt and steep influx of the island's foreign fauna, because some of the animals introduced to Mauritius, such as the monkey, goat, and wild boar, had been transported to the island by Portuguese sailors in previous years. Regardless of who brought them, though, these alien animals not only heightened the competition for food, water, and resources dramatically, many of them preyed on the dodo birds, which were severely inexperienced in terms of defense. The animals also devoured the precious, rare eggs of these hapless avians.

Adding to the problems, the swarms of disease-riddled rodents that scurried out of these ships may have infected substantial portions of the dodo bird population. Dodos lacked the natural immunization that could have shielded it from diseases found in faraway lands, so they were especially susceptible to these infections. The ardent planting of environmentally incompatible fruit trees and other foreign plants also damaged the dodo's habitat.

The marked spike in the construction of residential and industrial structures on the island, which meant the chopping of trees and clearing of the island's other vegetation, stripped the dodo birds of much of the resources they needed for survival. The Dutch settlers exploited the island's lavish supply of ebony trees, which were cut down, stacked onto ships, and sent to Batvia and Holland. Ebony trees were used in the crafting of a variety of colonial furniture, and their essence was bottled and sold as expensive fragrances. In later years, Mauritius ebony was also used in the production of sacred objects, musical instruments, and other trinkets such as statuettes and exquisite chess pieces.

The Dutch settlers could not plead ignorance to their reckless destruction of the island's resources. In 1650, the Batavian government, concerned about the potential exhaustion of the lucrative timber, attempted to install restrictions on the demolition of ebony trees in Mauritius. The number of ebony trees sawed down in a year, as stipulated by authorities, should not exceed 400. To the dismay of Batavian authorities, their fervent pleas fell on deaf ears. F. Rountree, author of *Some Aspects of Bird Life in Mauritius* (1951), explained, "During the Dutch occupation of the 17th century, all accessible ebony, and a great many other trees yielding good timber, were felled, and visiting Dutch vessels considerably reduced the number of edible palms, species of *Acantophoenix, Dictyosperma,* and *Latania* growing near the [Mauritius] coast."

The sugarcane, coffee, tobacco, rice, and indigo plantations that cropped up across the island in ensuing years added to the extensive damage suffered by the dodo bird's habitat.

Timber wasn't the only commodity that came back to Europe. In the early years of the 17th century, live dodo birds were brought back, contributing to the decline of the avian's fast-dwindling numbers. According to the calculations of Julian Pender Hume, a 21st century English paleontologist and author, at least 11 of the dodo birds that had been shipped overseas reached their destinations, and some believe that up to 17 birds made it to their ports of call alive. In 1610, Flemish painter and art extraordinaire Jakob Hoefnagel completed a collection of paintings that were commissioned by Holy Roman Emperor Rudolf II in Prague, and among the subjects was a dodo bird with chocolate brown and tan plumage, paired with beady, amber eyes and a black-tipped bill. It is believed to be the earliest known full-color painting of a dodo bird in Europe. The animal subjects in the Hoefnagel series were supposedly modeled after live specimens found in the emperor's private zoo, and Rudolf II's dodo bird may very well have been the first of its kind to be successfully exported from the island.

Hoefnagel's painting

Roelant Savery, another painter employed by the court of Holy Roman Emperor Rudolf II, tried his hand at painting the dodo in 1626, creating at least 10 different drawings of the avian altogether. Savery painted the bird after the deaths of both the emperor and his prized dodo, meaning that its depiction hinged on his memory, which led to a number of imprecisions. Savery may have also modeled his dodo, which was verging on obese, after stuffed dodos. Another possibility is that dodo birds in captivity may have been overfed and became bloated from a lack of exercise. Despite its faults, the most well-received of his paintings, entitled *Edwards' Dodo*, featured an all-gray dodo that reportedly belonged to ornithologist George Edwards, sandwiched between Mauritius red and gray parrots. It served as the stock image of the avian species for centuries.

Savery's painting of a dodo

That same year, the Dutch artist Adriaen van de Venne published his now controversial version of the dodo bird, a portly bird with a humped back and a bushy mass of feathers on its collar resting atop a pair of bent-back legs. De Venne's dodo bird was said to be a visual replica of a real dodo that he had encountered in Amsterdam, but whether it was alive or dead is uncertain. Moreover, modern viewers have noted it is awfully similar to Savery's depiction.

In 1628 and again in 1634, a British merchant trader and adventurer named Peter Mundy claimed to have happened upon two live dodo birds on display in Emperor Jahangir's menagerie in Surat, India. One of these dodos is believed to have served as a model for the legendary Mughal painter Ustad Mansur, who painted it three years prior. Like de Venne's dodo, Mansur's depiction of the bird had it adorned with tawny feathers dappled with shades of black, but it had a more slender torso, smaller white eyes, and it lacked the prominent hump seen in de Venne's rendition.

Mundy was struck by the remarkably offbeat appearance and unusual characteristics of the flightless bird, so much so that it led him to ponder the implications. In other words, he was considering the concepts of evolution and natural selection more than two centuries before Charles Darwin expounded on the revolutionary theory in his works. Regarding the dodo bird and the now extinct Mauritian red rail, *Aphanapetryx bonasia,* Mundry wrote, "Of these two sorts of fowl aforementioned, for ought we yet know, not any to be found out of this island, which lyeth about 100 leagues from St. Lawrence. A question may be demanded how they should be here and not elsewhere, being so far from motherland, and can neither fly [nor] swim; whether by mixture of kinds producing strange and mostrous formes, or the nature of the climate, air, and earth in altering the first shapes in long time, or how."

In June 1628, Essexshire-born author Emmanuel Althan mailed two letters to his brother, Sir Edward Altham, back home. In one of these letters, Emmanuel listed a variety of gifts that were pending departure in Mauritius, among which was a live dodo bird. Whether the dodo in question arrived in England alive is unknown, but part of Emmanuel's letter told his brother, "Most loving and kind brother, we were ordered by ye said council to go to an island called Mauritius, lying in 20 d. of south latitude, where we arrived in the 28th of May; this island having [sic] many goats, hogs, and cows upon it, and very strange fowls, called by ye portingalls 'Dodo,' which for the rareness of the same, the like being not in ye world but here. I have sent you one by Mr. Perce, who did arrive with the ship William at this island ye 10th of June." The scrawlings hastily squeezed into the margin of the letter added, "Of Mr. Perce you shall receive a jar of ginger for my sister, some beads for my cousins and your daughters, and a bird called a Dodo, if it live."

In 1634, Sir Thomas Herbert, a diplomat, historian, and the first English ambassador to the court of Persia, broke free from the norm when he published a description of the dodo in his book, *A Relation of Some Years Travel into Afrique and the Greater Asia.* His work cast the dodo in an unusually flattering light.

In addition to bearing eyes that gleamed like a pair of diamonds, the dodo, reportedly witnessed by Herbert during a trip to Mauritius in 1627, was cloaked in "downy feathers, her train three small plumes, short and inproportoinable [sic], [with] legs suiting her body, her pounces sharp, [and] her appetite strong and greedy." Herbert further noted, "[The dodo bird] is reputed more for wonder than for food, [as] greasy stomachs may seek after them, but to the delicate they are offensive and of no nourishment. Her visage darts forth melancholy, as sensible of Nature's injury in framing so great a body to be guided with complemental wings, so small and important, that they serve only to prove her bird..." Attached to this unorthodox profile of the dodo bird was a crude black-and-white illustration of the avian in question, which was presented next to a cacato and a hen to demonstrate its size.

Herbert's sketch

Four years later, English theologian, historian, and House of Commons representative Sir Hamon L'Estrange published a rambling entry about a live dodo bird he had admired in the flesh in London. This is considered to be the only substantiated account of a live dodo in Europe: "About 1638, as I walked London streets, I saw the picture of a strange looking fowl hung out upon a cloth, and myself with one or two more in company went in to see it. It was kept in a chamber, and was a great fowl somewhat bigger than the largest turkey cock, and so legged and footed, but stouter and thicker and of more erect shape, colored before like the breast of a young cock pheasant, and on the back of a dunn or dark color. The keeper called it a 'Dodo,' and in the end of a chimney in the chamber there lay a heap of large pebble stones, whereof he gave it many in our sight, some as big as nutmegs...the keeper told us that she eats them (conducing to digestion), and though I remember not how far the keeper was questioned therein, yet I am confident that afterwards she cast them all again."

In 1647, a dodo bird was exported all the way to Nagasaki, and it is believed to be the last known dodo kept in captivity.

Too Little, Too Late

"These animals on our coming up to them stared at us and remained quiet where they stand, not knowing whether they had wings to fly away or legs to run off, and suffering us to approach them as close as we pleased. Amongst these birds were those which in India they call Dod-aersen (being a kind of very big goose); these birds are unable to fly, and instead of wings, they merely have a few small pins, yet they can run very swiftly. We drove them together into one place in such a manner that we could catch them with our hands, and when we held one of them by its leg, and that upon this it made a great noise, the others all on a sudden came running as fast as they could to its assistance, and by which they were caught and made prisoners also." - Volkert Evertsz, a Dutch mariner

Unfortunately, the private collectors and exhibition operators who exported and displayed dodo birds in the mid-17th century were some of the last people in history to be graced with the dodo bird's presence. Although the concept of extinction did not yet exist, by 1662, the dodo birds had been classified a species that could no longer be found in its homeland on Mauritius. The honor of witnessing the last confirmed dodo birds on the island – more specifically on an islet in Mauritius now known as "Amber Island" – belonged to a Dutch mariner named Volkert Evertsz. He described the almost effortless techniques they employed to capture these overly trusting, unworldly creatures. Other birds embarked on a suicide mission to come to the aid of the targeted dodo birds, only to find themselves ensnarled in the trap in the process. Evertsz's account would go on to play a vital role in shaping the dodo bird's enduring, yet erroneous reputation.

Of course, determining the exact date of the dodo bird's extinction is a complex task to say the least, and naturally, it is a subject of intense debate. While Everetsz's account certainly came at a time when dodo birds were on the brink of extinction, some say that a resilient few managed to survive at least three more decades.

Over the next 30 years, a number of reports pertaining to alleged sightings of the increasingly elusive birds surfaced. Apart from the historical documents published in 1673, which chronicled the slaughter of a flock of dodo birds that were presented to Governor Hugo, reports of two separate dodo sightings between the years of 1663 and 1674 emerged. The reports were narrated by a 25-year-old runaway slave known only as "Simon," who had recently been recaptured. The fact that the "fugitive" had only spotted the dodo bird twice throughout his 11 years in hiding further underscores the bird's critically endangered status. Some have advised readers of Simon's report to take his statements with a grain of salt, since Simon may have been desperate to get into his captors' good graces and thus simply fabricated these sightings. That said, other reports claimed to have seen dodo birds in the years after Simon, so there may have been some credibility in his accounts after all.

In 1681, Benjamin Harry, a scientist and first mate aboard the ship *Berkeley Castle*, became the last Briton to encounter a live dodo bird. Today, Harry is most renowned for being the first individual to effectively measure the angle of the Earth's magnetic field across the Southern Hemisphere. No doubt oblivious of this sobering reality, he wrote of the experience, "Now having a little respite, I will make a little description: of ye island first of its Producks and yns of its parts – first of winged and fathered fowle ye less passant, are Dodos whose flesh is very hard, a small sort of Geese reasona..."

Again, the claims made in Harry's report that couldn't be substantiated were initially brushed off and filed away as anecdotal, and cynicism continues to hover over Harry's account to this day. Among the modern skeptics is a prolific author and independent ornithologist by the name of Anthony Cheke, who unreservedly believed that the dodo bird met its demise in 1662. As maintained by Cheke, the species had already been wiped out in Mauritius by the 1660s, and the last sightings that followed, according to Cheke, were no more than cases of mistaken identity. Cheke thus asserted the "dodos" mentioned in these reports were most likely red rails, and that Harry's report, while inaccurate, was backed by good intentions. As Cheke put it, "[His] ability as an observer is not the issue. He saw or ate a bird he was told by the locals was a 'dodo,' and naturally that's what he called it in his account. This does not make him 'unreliable.'"

Governor Hugo's successor, Opperhoofd Isaac Joan Lamotius, continued to make references on at least a dozen different occasions to the allegedly extant dodos on Mauritius in the journals that he kept between the years of 1685 and 1688. Lamotious' "last sighting" of the dodo bird, also on Amber Island, purportedly came on November 25, 1688. Like Cheke, skeptics insist that the avians Lamotious had come across were red rails. Having said that, one must take into consideration Lamotious' stellar reputation as an "observer of nature," one who would have been unlikely to make such an amateurish mistake.

Other reports claimed that the dodo birds that somehow wound up in isolated coastal areas of Mauritius, as well as neighboring Mascarene Islands, remained in those parts until they faded out of existence in the 1690s. A study conducted by A. R. Solow and D. L. Roberts in 2003, wordily entitled "A Nonparametric Test for Extinction Based on a Sighting Record," narrowed down the dodo bird's date of extinction to approximately 1693 via the "Weibull distribution method," which was supported by a "95% confidence interval [in regard to its date of extinction]" in the years between 1688 and 1715.

Whenever it happened, the dodo birds were extinct around the late 17th century or early 18th century, and this haunting notion was only fully grasped by scientists and the public alike in the early 19th century thanks to the French naturalist and zoologist Georges Cuvier, who helped people understand the meaning of extinction in 1796. Even then, extinction remained an alien idea even within scientific circles until the late 18th century, so scientists and collectors were utterly careless in their handling of the now coveted dodo bird specimens. Those who were fortunate enough to come into contact with the actual remnants of these birds had only a shallow understanding of preservation techniques, and they wrongfully assumed that dodo remains, while undoubtedly valuable, would be easily replaced. In reality, the tropical, humid climate of Mauritius accelerated the decay of corpses, as opposed to the freezing temperatures in Siberia, which boasted a nursery of exquisitely well-preserved mammoth fossils encased in permafrost.

Moreover, the fields of taxidermy and record-keeping were only in their fledgling stages, which meant that the loss of bones and the inadvertent damage inflicted upon many of them were commonplace.

Taxidermists began to produce stuffed dodo carcasses as early as the first decade of the 17th century, but most, if not all of these specimens eventually vanished over time, leaving no traces behind. One such specimen, supposedly derived from Warwijck and van Neck's pioneering voyage, that managed to avoid this fate was a "dried dodo foot" that belonged to a man named Pieter Pauw, the Primary Professor of Medicine at the University of Leiden in Holland. An acclaimed Artois doctor and botanist, Carolus Clusius, who coined the dodo bird's first scientific name, *Gallinaceus Gallus peregrinus,* described the foot in vivid detail in a report published in 1605: "After I put together and described as faithfully as I could the history of this bird, I happened to see its leg cut off as far as the knee, at the house of that most illustrious man (Pieter Pauw), recently brought out of Mauritius Island. It was but not very long, from the knee all the way to the bending of the foot a little more than four inches only; its thickness, however, was great, being almost four inches in circumference, and was covered in thick skin as scales, in the front part wider and yellow, on the back, however, smaller and dusky. Besides the upper part of the toes was also furnished with broad single scales, but on the back these were totally callous, and the toes were short enough for such a thick leg..." Sadly, Pauw failed to keep the dried bird foot within his reach, and little else is known about its ultimate fate.

In 1634, two separate reports, both of which featured short passages alluding to dodo bird remnants that had been transferred to the Oxford School of Anatomy, were published. The first, authored by Thomas Crosfield, was more vague in its reference to the avian, describing the carcass as that of a "black Indian bird." The second passage, printed in the institution's 1634 catalog, was a concise caption describing a "Couple of Dodoes [sic]." Like their supposed albino equivalents, all-black dodo birds did not exist, so the darkness of the "black Indian bird" was most likely the discolored carcass of a badly decomposed dodo.

In 1656, what was then the best-preserved and most complete dodo carcass to date found its way into the open arms of trailblazing gardener and naturalist John Tradescant the Elder, the proprietor of Musaeum Tradescantianum, London's first public museum. The dodo was part of Tradescant's collection of historical curiosities exhibited in the Lambeth institution, and underneath it was a brass plate identifying the species as "a *dodar* from the island of Mauritius." Tradescant's entire collection, as well as the museum itself, was later inherited by his son, John Tradescant the Younger. To this day, experts have yet to agree on the identity of Tradescant's dodo. Most believe it was the dodo encountered by Sir L'Estrange in London 18 years prior, but some say it was the bird that Altham had shipped to his brother. Still others think it was a generous donation courtesy of Thomas Herbert.

John Tradescant the Elder

When Tradescant the Younger died suddenly in April of 1662, the original Tradescant collection, including the dodo specimen, was bequeathed to his close personal friend, Elias Ashmole. The collection, under Ashmole's orders, was relocated to the Ashmolean Museum (now the Ashmolean Museum of Art and Archaeology) in Oxford, the world's first museum built within a university campus, upon the completion of its first building in 1678. Here, the dodo specimen, by this time nicknamed the "Oxford Dodo," remained enshrined until 1755, when the museum's board members declared the half-rotted carcass an eyesore and had it removed from the exhibit. According to a persistent rumor, the board members were so revolted by the putrid stench wafting from the moldering dodo corpse that they ordered the museum hands to chuck the entire specimen into a roaring bonfire. The dodo would have been reduced to an unrecognizable pile of ashes and charred leftovers had it not been for an astute unidentified naturalist, who wrested the dodo skull and one of its feet out of the flames in the nick of time.

While this certainly makes for a thrilling story, museum operators say this is nothing more than an apocryphal anecdote. In reality, the removal of the Oxford Dodo was intended to be a temporary arrangement, and its skull and foot were the only articles that could be salvaged from its extreme state of decomposition. The head and foot of the original Tradescant specimen continues to be housed in Oxford's University Museum of Zoology to this day.

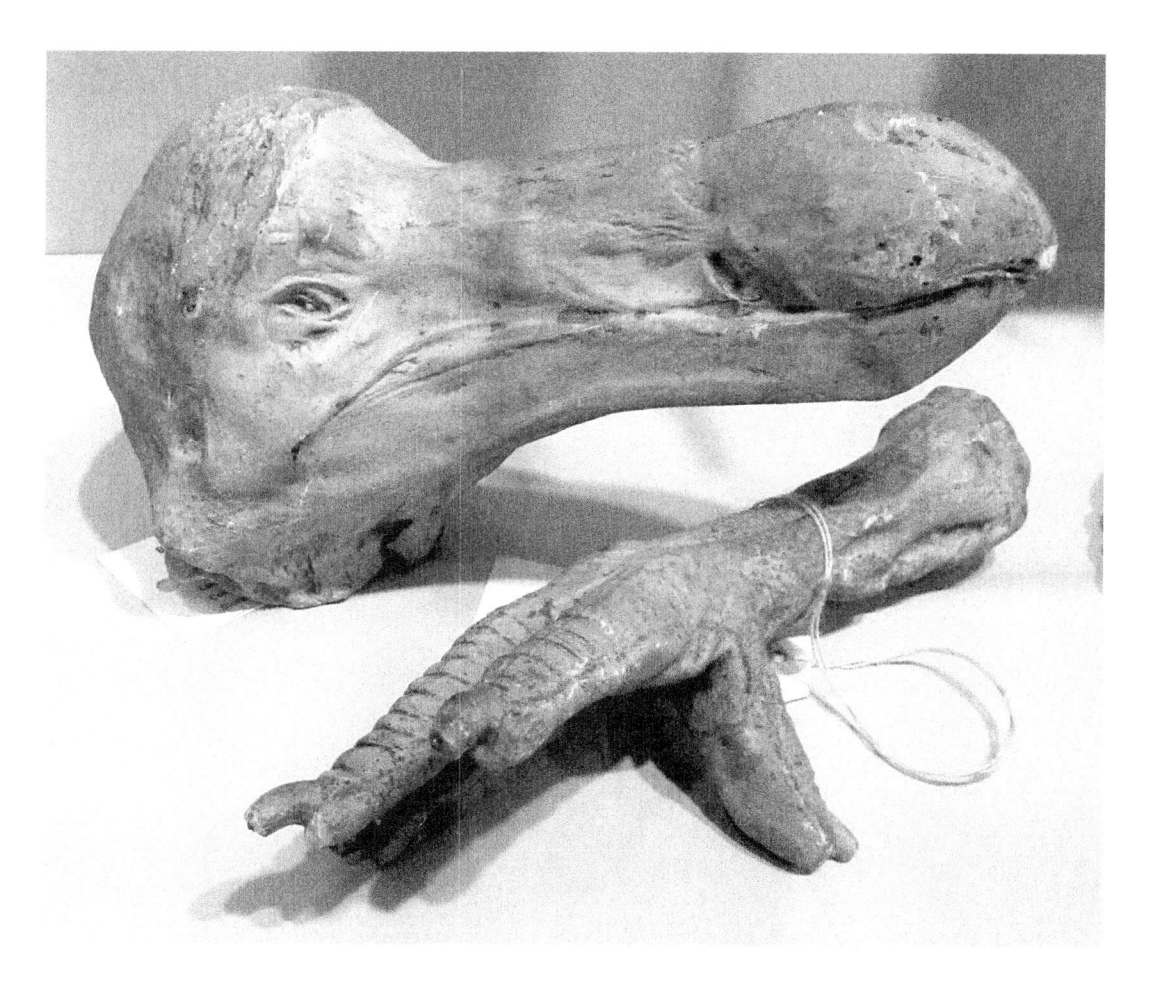

Michael Romanov's picture of a plaster cast of the Oxford dodo's head and foot

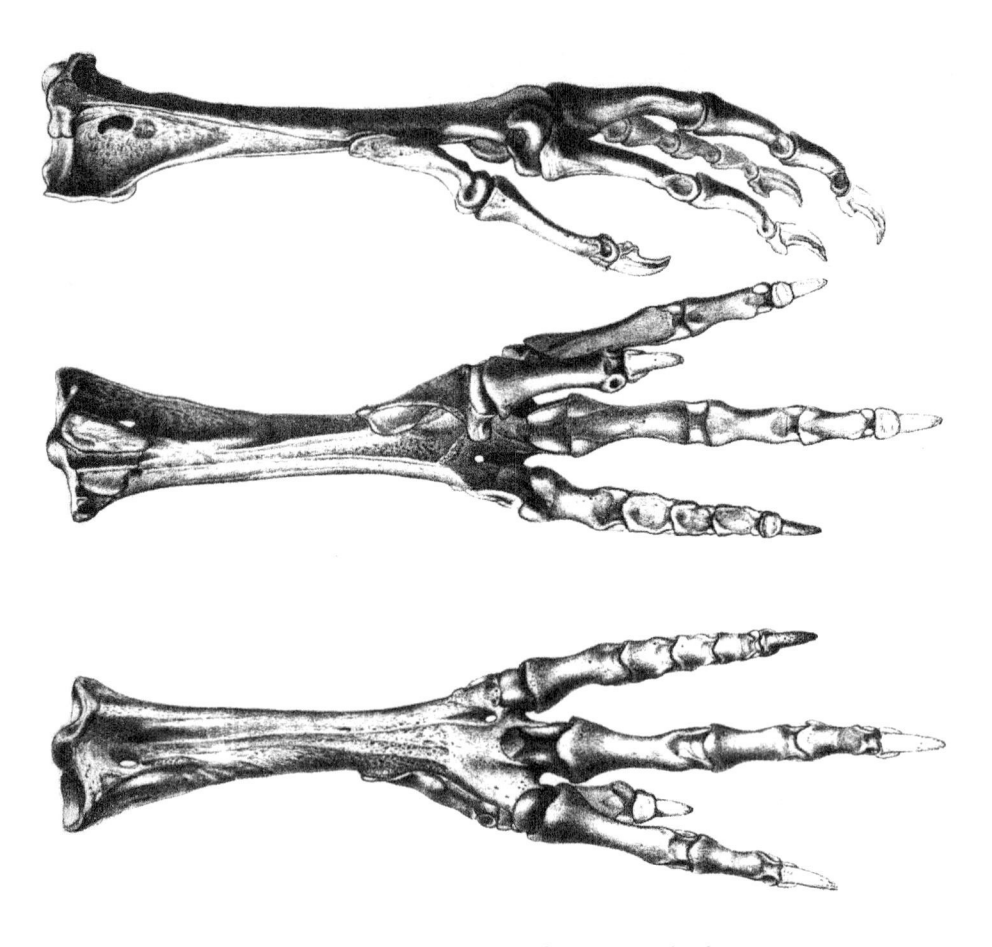

A lithograph of the Oxford dodo's foot

In April 2018, scientists around the world were amazed when the Oxford dodo's cause of death was determined. A chain of CT scans and a 3D reproduction of the bird conducted by Professor Paul Smith, director of the Museum of Natural History, and Professor Mark William of Warwick University revealed that the dodo had been killed by a shotgun blast to the back of the skull. The shotgun was fired at close range, which probably served as the accelerant to its rapid deterioration. Smith explained, "We found a strange cluster of metallic flakes and particles. We thought at first it was contaminated. [Then] we pulled out a pellet. It looked like lead, and lo and behold it was analyzed and it was a lead pellet. In our wildest dreams, we never expected to find what we did."

The 2018 findings definitively put the rumors regarding the original owners of the Oxford dodo to rest, and the Oxford dodo remains the only soft tissue specimen of its kind in existence.

A second dried dodo bird foot, referred to as either the "British Museum" or "London Foot," was donated to the Royal Society in the early 18th century following its discovery in 1665. The foot was later transferred to the British Museum (now the Natural History Museum), hence its nickname. The hind toes of the dehydrated appendage were positioned at right angles in relation to the foot, which implies that the foot had been a "fresh" amputation, either from a dying, but still breathing bird, or one that was recently deceased. The London Foot was displayed alongside Savery's *Edwards' Dodo* in the avian exhibit of the British Museum until 1848. Sadly, the exact whereabouts of the London Foot today are unknown.

Lessons Learned

"We don't kill unless threatened.

Did you not perceive the Dutchmen as a threat?

Yet he has no choice...

the bird replied, foraging, head down,

Diamond eyes shrunken to slits

As it pried grubs from mud..." - Judish Skillman, "The Dodo Bird"

By the early 19th century, dodo birds had been exhibited in various museums across England for well over a century, but the avian only intrigued the British Victorian masses after the 1833 publication of a riveting disquisition in a local magazine founded by the Society of the Diffusion of Useful Knowledge. It appears that even then, people were aware of the role they played in the dodo bird's extinction. An excerpt from the article, simply entitled "The Dodo," found in the June 1, 1833 edition of *Penny Magazine*, told readers, "The agency of man, in limiting the increase of the inferior animals and in extirpating certain races was perhaps never more strikingly exemplified than in the case of the dodo. That a species so remarkable in its character should become extinct, within little more than two centuries, so that the fact of its existence at all has been doubted, is a circumstance which may well excite our surprise, and lead us to a consideration of similar changes which are still going on from the same cause..."

In 1860, a British physician and botanist named Philip Burnard Ayres secured his own page in the history books when he uncovered the first known sub-fossil (partially fossilized remnants) of a dodo bird in Mauritius. Rather than let the historic specimen sit around and collect dust, Ayres entrusted the remnants to the care of the arrogant, but undeniably brilliant Richard Owen, founder of the British Museum and the first to coin the word "dinosaur." While it would have been safe to assume that such a find would make the rest of the scientific community take notice, no one outside of the museum heard a peep from Owen, who deliberately decided against publicizing Ayres' findings. Three years later, a Mauritian bishop named Vincent Ryan was instructed to discreetly alert Owen of any new dodo bird findings on the island.

Owen pictured with a crocodile skull

Paleontologists burrowed through the rusty red Mauritian ground for the next 24 months, with streams of sweat cascading down their backs and dripping from their hairlines, but not a single dodo bird remnant was found. The bad luck finally ended in 1865 with a group of laborers who had been tasked with laying down a network of railway tracks that would lead to one of the island's sugar plantations. As the story goes, the observant railway engineer presiding over the project cottoned on to a new trend that had taken shape amongst the laborers. The railway workers, he observed, had begun to frequent a particularly marshy pit in the area, where they appeared to be fishing for bones. The bones they pocketed were later crushed and sprinkled over the soil of their own personal farms, supposedly as a helpful fertilizer.

After seeing that, the railway engineer collected a few bones himself and brought them over to a local schoolmaster at Mahebourg named George Clark. Clark seemed to recognize the bones and their source at once, the latter of which is now referred to as the "Mare aux Songes swamp" in southern Mauritius. The swamp first came into prominence in the scientific world back in 1832 because it was apparently so rich in fossils that one only had to lightly skim their fingers across the murky surface to touch an animal bone. Clark made a beeline for the swamp and proceeded to unearth hundreds of individual dodo bird bone fragments, now believed to have been approximately 4,000 years in age. By the end of the year, a few sets of nearly complete dodo skeletons sourced from the swamp were shipped to Great Britain. Curators at the British Museum purchased 100 of these sub-fossils, forking over a pound for each bone fragment. Leftover pieces of dodo skeletons were auctioned off in the capital in the spring of 1866. That same year, Owen published the first fully realized monograph of a dodo bird skeleton, which he based on the dodo sub-fossils retrieved from different parts of Mauritius.

As groundbreaking as this work was, Owen's publication was beset by layers of scandal. To begin with, his version of the dodo skeleton was chiefly modeled after Savery's overly porky and anatomically inaccurate dodo painting. The inconsistencies were eventually righted in 1872, with the new model bearing a thinner neck and a less-pronounced breast.

Owen's envious peers in the scientific community were appalled by the overtly self-serving tactics he employed to acquire the specimens needed for his work, which included his refusal to award credit where it was due. Owen, for instance, was said to have swooped down on a shipment of dodo sub-fossils that had originally been addressed to Alfred Newton, another anatomist tenured at the University of Cambridge. This sparked something of a rivalry between the two scientists, and in the end, Newton realized that the resources provided to him by the university were overshadowed by those readily available at the British Museum. Thus, he set aside his ego and relented, allowing Owen complete and unobstructed ownership of the dodo remnants.

Newton

In the early 20th century, Louis Etienne Thirioux, a Port-Louis-based hairdresser by day and amateur naturalist by night, assembled one of the most comprehensive private collections of dodo bird fossils ever known. The colorfully diverse assortment comprised of a variety of dodo components, as well as "partially articulated specimens," which included a skeleton now considered to be the most "articulated" of all of the dodo remnants ever uncovered outside of the Mare aux Songes swamp. In later years, Thirioux offered up his outstandingly unique collection for sale, in particular casting his bait in Newton's direction. Newton, unfortunately, did not nibble, and he insulted Thirioux in the process when he deemed the collection to be worth no more than a measly £20. The value of Thirioux's dodo specimens were only acknowledged after his death. One of Thirioux's dodo skeletons is now exhibited at the Durban Natural Science Museum in South Africa, and another at the Natural History Museum in Port-Louis.

The fascination with dodo birds reached a fevered pitch in the 19th century, but it eventually petered out as the 20th century progressed, and it remained in a state of relative dormancy until Christmas Day in 2005. A masterly team of researchers staffed with leading scientists from around the globe exhumed a trove of dodo fossils at an abandoned sugarcane plantation, which included 17 individual dodo specimens in different stages of maturity, most of which ranged between 2,000 and 3,000 years in age. Kenneth Rijsdijk, the Dutch geologist who led the excavations, reported, "We have found 700 bones including bones from 20 dodo birds and chicks, and we [still] believe there are many more at the site."

The following year, scientists stumbled upon the complete skeleton of a dodo bird buried within a lava cave on Mauritius Island; only the second skeleton belonging to an individual bird that has ever been recovered. In September 2019, scientists hit the jackpot again with the discovery of yet another stash of dodo bones, estimated to be roughly 12,000 years old, stowed away in an unexplored region of the Mare aux Songes swamp. Dr. J.P. Hume, who was appropriately exhilarated by the find, described the discovery as "one of the most exciting fossil excavations [he had] ever worked on." In addition to the mass of dodo bird fossils, remnants of extinct giant tortoises and giant skinks were recovered at the site.

Unlike most other creatures who have fallen victim to extinction, one can confidently ascribe the disappearance of the dodo bird to both the direct and indirect intervention of humans. Today, the dodo bird, now the main mascot of the island nation of Mauritius, has been established as the perennial poster child for extinction, offering up a sad lesson in the lasting, infectious, and often disastrous ripple effects that arise from the careless and short-sighted actions of mankind.

In fact, the dodo bird was hardly the only victim. Of the 45 bird species that were originally found across Mauritius, only 21 species have managed to survive, a concerning figure that is still in danger of slipping. Scientists estimate that if the current trajectory continues, the world might lose up to 25% of all avian species across the board in less than 100 years.

Online Resources

Other books about ancient history by Charles River Editors

Other books about the dodo on Amazon

Bibliography

Anthes, E. (2016, June 8). The Smart, Agile, and Completely Underrated Dodo. Retrieved December 27, 2019, from https://www.theatlantic.com/science/archive/2016/06/the-dodos-redemption/486086/.

Barras, C. (2016, April 9). How Humanity Killed the First Dodo and Lost It As Well. Retrieved December 27, 2019, from http://www.bbc.com/earth/story/20160408-how-humanity-first-killed-the-dodo-then-lost-it-as-well.

Black, A. (2013, November 19). Alice, Oxford, and the Dodo. Retrieved December 27, 2019, from https://www.atlasobscura.com/articles/alice-oxford-and-the-dodo.

Bodio, S. J. (2014, April 15). A Tale Of Three Superdoves: The Dodo, The Rock Pigeon, And The Passenger Pigeon. Retrieved December 27, 2019, from https://www.allaboutbirds.org/news/a-tale-of-three-superdoves-the-dodo-the-rock-pigeon-and-the-passenger-pigeon/.

Borschberg, P. (2015). *Journal, Memorials and Letters of Cornelis Matelieff de Jonge: Security, Diplomacy and Commerce in 17th-century Southeast Asia*. NUS Press.

Brown, B. S. (2002). Raphus cucullatus dodo. Retrieved December 27, 2019, from https://animaldiversity.org/accounts/Raphus_cucullatus/.

Charlton, M. (2018, December 4). What the Dodo Means to Mauritius. Retrieved December 27, 2019, from https://www.atlasobscura.com/articles/mauritius-and-the-dodo.

Claro, V. (2017). Shipwrecks, Treasures, and Divers. Retrieved December 27, 2019, from https://www.mysterra.org/webmag/mauritius/shipwrecks.html.

Cowan, L. (2016, April 14). Memoir on the Dodo. Retrieved December 27, 2019, from http://blogs.reading.ac.uk/special-collections/2016/04/memoir-on-the-dodo/.

Davis, N. (2017, August 24). Life cycle of the mysterious and long-dead dodo revealed by bone study. Retrieved December 27, 2019, from https://www.theguardian.com/science/2017/aug/24/life-cycle-of-the-mysterious-and-long-dead-dodo-revealed-by-bone-study.

Derbyshire, D. (2003, November 20). Scientists pinpoint last days of the dodo. Retrieved December 27, 2019, from https://www.telegraph.co.uk/news/science/science-news/3315646/Scientists-pinpoint-last-days-of-the-dodo.html.

Editors, A. N. (2018). Dodo. Retrieved December 27, 2019, from https://animals.net/dodo/.

Editors, B. (2019, September). Dodo Bird. Retrieved December 27, 2019, from https://www.bagheera.com/dodo-bird/.

Editors, B. S. (2019, August 17). The dodo tree and other stories. Retrieved December 27, 2019, from https://stories.rbge.org.uk/archives/19390.

Editors, D. B. (2017). HISTORY OF THE DODO BIRD. Retrieved December 27, 2019, from https://www.dodobird.net/dodo-bird-history.

Editors, E. A. (2015, July 28). Dodo Bird. Retrieved December 27, 2019, from https://www.extinctanimals.org/dodo-bird.htm.

Editors, F. C. (2015, February 18). Dodo Bird Facts. Retrieved December 27, 2019, from https://facts.net/nature/animals/dodo-bird-facts.

Editors, H. D. (2018, September 7). Dodo Birds – A Misunderstood Extinction Story. Retrieved December 27, 2019, from https://historydaily.org/dodo-birds-a-misunderstood-extinction-story.

Editors, I. (2006, June 9). Driven to extinction: Who killed the Dodo? Retrieved December 27, 2019, from https://www.independent.co.uk/news/science/driven-to-extinction-who-killed-the-dodo-481631.html.

Editors, M. A. (2018). Mauritius Dodo. Retrieved December 27, 2019, from https://mauritiusattractions.com/mauritius-dodo-i-102.html.

Editors, M. N. (2018). The Oxford Dodo. Retrieved December 27, 2019, from https://oumnh.ox.ac.uk/the-oxford-dodo.

Editors, M. A. (2018). Mauritius History. Retrieved December 27, 2019, from https://mauritiusattractions.com/mauritius-history-i-79.html.

Editors, N. W. (2008, April 3). Dodo. Retrieved December 27, 2019, from https://www.newworldencyclopedia.org/entry/Dodo.

Editors, N. G. (2011, December 12). Repost: The Dodo is Dead, Long Live the Dodo! Retrieved December 27, 2019, from https://www.nationalgeographic.com/science/phenomena/2011/12/12/repost-the-dodo-is-dead-long-live-the-dodo/.

Editors, R. M. (2016). Everything You Ever Wanted to Know About the Dodo . Retrieved December 27, 2019, from https://artsandculture.google.com/theme/everything-you-ever-wanted-to-know-about-the-dodo /lQKCJWtqLgvEIA?hl=en.

Editors, T. M. (2014). PIETER BOTH. Retrieved December 27, 2019, from https://www.trekkingmauritius.com/pieter-both/.

Editors, T. T. (2019, December 10). Dumb Dodo Bird. Retrieved December 27, 2019, from https://tvtropes.org/pmwiki/pmwiki.php/Main/DumbDodoBird.

Editors, U. U. (2012). The dodos of Clusius and Van de Venne: true to life or not? Retrieved December 27, 2019, from https://bc.library.uu.nl/dodos-clusius-and-van-de-venne-true-life-or-not.html.

Editors, U. W. (2018, April 21). Dodo's violent death revealed. Retrieved December 27, 2019, from https://www.sciencedaily.com/releases/2018/04/180421180509.htm.

Editors, W. (2019, December 26). Dodo. Retrieved December 27, 2019, from https://en.wikipedia.org/wiki/Dodo.

Editors, W. (2019, June 16). Dodo (Alice's Adventures in Wonderland). Retrieved December 27, 2019, from https://en.wikipedia.org/wiki/Dodo_(Alice's_Adventures_in_Wonderland).

Editors, W. (2019, September 7). Jacob Corneliszoon van Neck. Retrieved December 27, 2019, from https://en.wikipedia.org/wiki/Jacob_Corneliszoon_van_Neck.

Editors, W. (2019, January 31). File:Jacht op dodo's door Willem van West-Zanen uit 1602.jpg. Retrieved December 27, 2019, from https://commons.wikimedia.org/wiki/File:Jacht_op_dodo's_door_Willem_van_West-Zanen_uit_1602.jpg.

Gandhi, M. S. (2017, December 30). Animal- Human Hybrid in Mythology and Folklore. Retrieved December 27, 2019, from https://www.newdelhitimes.com/animal-human-hybrid-in-mythology-and-folklore/.

Glowatz, E. (2018, April 20). FAMOUS DODO SAID TO HAVE INSPIRED 'ALICE IN WONDERLAND' CHARACTER DIED AFTER IT WAS SHOT IN HEAD. Retrieved December 27, 2019, from https://www.newsweek.com/famous-dodo-murdered-shot-back-species-went-extinct-895302.

Greer, P. (2019, March 14). DRAWINGS OF DODO'S (GENERALLY ASSUMED FROM TO BE LIFE) BY JORIS JOOSTENSZ LAERLE (1601) & CORNELIS SAFTLEVEN (1638). Retrieved December 27, 2019, from https://paulgreer.net/2019/03/14/drawings-of-dodos-generally-assumed-from-to-be-life-by-joris-joostensz-laerle-1601-cornelis-saftleven-1638/.

Hamill, J. (2018, April 20). Mystery of 'Alice in Wonderland' Dodo murdered 350 years ago is finally solved. Retrieved December 27, 2019, from https://metro.co.uk/2018/04/20/mystery-alice-wonderland-dodo-murdered-350-years-ago-finally-solved-7483435/.

Holmberg, L. (2012, May 23). Mauritius. A study in disaster. Retrieved December 27, 2019, from https://www.tandfonline.com/doi/pdf/10.1080/00708852.1962.10418985.

Hume, J., & Cheke, A. (2004, April). The white dodo of Réunion Island: unravelling a scientific and historical myth. Retrieved December 27, 2019, from https://www.researchgate.net/publication/289502850_The_white_dodo_of_Reunion_Island_unravelling_a_scientific_and_historical_myth.

Hume, J. (2006). The history of the Dodo Raphus cucullatus and the penguin of Mauritius. Retrieved December 27, 2019, from https://www.academia.edu/7702952/The_history_of_the_Dodo_Raphus_cucullatus_and_the_penguin_of_Mauritius.

Khalid, W. (2014, August 7). Dodo Bird Facts | Top 10 Interesting Facts about Dodo Bird. Retrieved December 27, 2019, from https://animalstime.com/dodo-bird-facts-top-10-interesting-facts-about-dodo-bird/.

Khalifa, A. (2019, July 12). "DEAF AS…" | A LIST OF 30 DEAF IDIOMS & THEIR ORIGINS. Retrieved December 27, 2019, from https://hearmeoutcc.com/deaf-as-idioms/#idiom10.

Kiberd, R. (2015, March 18). The Dodo Didn't Look Like You Think It Does. Retrieved December 27, 2019, from https://www.vice.com/en_us/article/vvbqq9/the-dodo-didnt-look-like-you-think-it-does.

Main, D. (2013, October 9). When did the dodo go extinct? Maybe later than we thought. Retrieved December 27, 2019, from https://www.nbcnews.com/sciencemain/when-did-dodo-go-extinct-maybe-later-we-thought-8C11361418.

Main, D. (2013, October 9). When did the dodo go extinct? Maybe later than we thought. Retrieved December 27, 2019, from https://www.nbcnews.com/sciencemain/when-did-dodo-go-extinct-maybe-later-we-thought-8C11361418.

Meek, J. (2002, March 1). Dodo's DNA points the finger at Nicobar pigeon. Retrieved December 27, 2019, from https://www.theguardian.com/uk/2002/mar/01/books.research.

Milliken, G. (2016, February 25). Dodos Were Actually Not That Dumb. Retrieved December 27, 2019, from https://www.popsci.com/dodos-were-smarter-than-we-thought/.

Moss, S. (2002, December 14). Gone but not forgotten. Retrieved December 27, 2019, from https://www.theguardian.com/books/2002/dec/14/scienceandnature.highereducation.

Parish, J. C. (2013). *The Dodo and the Solitaire: A Natural History*. Indiana University Press.

Parker, I. (2017, January 14). Digging for Dodos. Retrieved December 27, 2019, from https://www.newyorker.com/magazine/2007/01/22/digging-for-dodos.

Pavid, K. (2019, September 12). A 12,000-year-old swamp full of dodo bones has been found. Retrieved December 27, 2019, from https://www.nhm.ac.uk/discover/news/2019/september/swamp-full-of-dodo-bones-found.html.

Piet, D. (2010). *Mauritius on the Spice Route, 1598-1810*. Editions Didier Millet.

Pinto-Correia, C. (2006). *Return of the Crazy Bird: The Sad, Strange Tale of the Dodo*. Springer Science & Business Media.

Pistorius, M. (2017, December 1). Mauritius: From Conquests to Naval Battles, Piracy and a Long-Awaited Independence. Retrieved December 27, 2019, from https://www.ancient-origins.net/history-important-events/mauritius-conquests-naval-battles-piracy-and-long-awaited-independence-021738.

Pruitt, S. (2018, August 31). Scientists Say Lost Ancient Continent Lies Beneath Island in Indian Ocean. Retrieved December 27, 2019, from https://www.history.com/news/scientists-say-lost-ancient-continent-lies-beneath-island-in-indian-ocean.

Roberts, D. L., & Solow, A. R. (2003, November 20). When did the dodo become extinct? Retrieved December 27, 2019, from https://www.nature.com/articles/426245a.

Smallwood, K. (2013, June 28). WHY THE DODO WENT EXTINCT. Retrieved December 27, 2019, from http://www.todayifoundout.com/index.php/2013/06/why-the-dodo-went-extinct/.

Sterling, B. (2005, December 25). Dodo bird bones found on island. Retrieved December 27, 2019, from https://www.ocregister.com/2005/12/25/dodo-bird-bones-found-on-island/.

Strauss, B. (2018, September 21). 10 Facts About the Dodo Bird. Retrieved December 27, 2019, from https://www.thoughtco.com/facts-about-the-dodo-bird-1092144.

Strickland, A. (2017, August 24). What you didn't know about the dodo. Retrieved December 27, 2019, from https://edition.cnn.com/2017/08/24/world/dodo-extinct-new-insight/index.html.

Than, K. (2013, February 27). Ancient Lost Continent Discovered in Indian Ocean. Retrieved December 27, 2019, from https://www.nationalgeographic.com/news/2013/2/130225-microcontinent-earth-mauritius-geology-science/.

Charles Knight. (1833). *The Penny Magazine of the Society for the Diffusion of Useful Knowledge, 第2卷*.

Young, L. (2016, May 20). The Scientific Squabble Over the Dodo Tree. Retrieved December 27, 2019, from https://www.atlasobscura.com/articles/the-scientific-squabble-over-the-dodo-tree.

Free Books by Charles River Editors

We have brand new titles available for free most days of the week. To see which of our titles are currently free, click on this link.

Discounted Books by Charles River Editors

We have titles at a discount price of just 99 cents everyday. To see which of our titles are currently 99 cents, click on this link.

Printed in Great Britain
by Amazon